DOLPHIN LANGUAGE

By Jay Leibold
Illustrated by Pat Traub

D1301029

Macmillan McGraw-Hill

New York   Farmington

Imagine you are swimming in a calm, blue ocean. You put your head under water. You hear whistles and clicks all around you. Suddenly, *ping*—a small shock goes through your body.

A flash of gray and white whips past you. You turn to see a six-foot-long creature with gentle brown eyes looking straight at you. The corners of its mouth are turned up in what seems to be a smile. You could swear this creature is thinking about you. It might even know something about you that you don't know.

People have had special feelings about dolphins for thousands of years. Watching them dive and play in the ocean, we wonder what is going on in their brains. Dolphins seem to be curious about people, too. They will come to shore to look at bathers on the beach. They will follow boats for miles. There has always been a special connection between humans and these sleek, graceful marine animals.

Dolphins are mammals, just as we are. They need to breathe air and keep their body at a certain temperature. Their normal life span is anywhere from twenty to forty years. They are related to porpoises, sperm whales and white whales, and narwhals. All of them belong to the order *Cetacea*. Sometimes dolphins are called the "littlest whale." But these little whales can weigh four to five hundred pounds!

Dolphins have no sense of smell, but they have a sense of taste and good eyesight. Their soft and slippery skin is very sensitive to touch.

Long ago, people believed dolphins were humans who had returned to the sea. Today we know that is not true. But it *is* true that dolphins once lived on land. They were hairy mammals with long tails. They walked on four legs. Later, their front feet evolved into flippers.

For many years people have kept dolphins in captivity. Trainers teach dolphins to perform tricks in aquatic shows and to play parts in movies. Their special qualities are put to commercial use.

However, our ideas about dolphins are starting to change. We are thinking more deeply about their world. Many people enjoy swimming alongside dolphins in their natural marine environment. Scientists are listening very carefully to the way dolphins speak.

Dolphins have been on earth for 65 million years longer than humans. Their brains are bigger than ours. This is why some scientists think dolphins are the most advanced creatures on Earth and that they may have a thing or two to tell us.

Whistles, clicks, and barks! Yelps, moans, and grunts! Squawks and wails! Dolphins love to talk, but what on earth are they saying?

Each dolphin has a personal whistle that identifies it to other dolphins. A baby dolphin's whistle is wobbly at first, but soon becomes clear and strong.

A baby will whistle to its mother in dark water to let her know where it is. The whistle identifies both the mother and the baby, as though to say, "Hey Mom, it's me, Opo, over here!" If the baby is in trouble, its whistle becomes higher and louder.

When a dolphin whistles, another dolphin will answer. In this way they will always know who is nearby. If dolphins swimming in a school get hungry, they will whistle more often. They seem to be calling back and forth to try to get the others to go on a hunt. They continue to whistle as they chase after a tasty fish dinner.

It appears that everyone in the whale family speaks a related language. When swimming near other types of dolphins or whales, dolphins can identify the other group by their whistles. A small bottlenose dolphin can exchange a few whistles with a giant sperm whale.

Besides whistling, dolphins make a lot of other sounds. They squeak like a creaky door, squawk like a parrot, quack like a duck, and even bark like a dog. This "language" has been dubbed "delphinese."

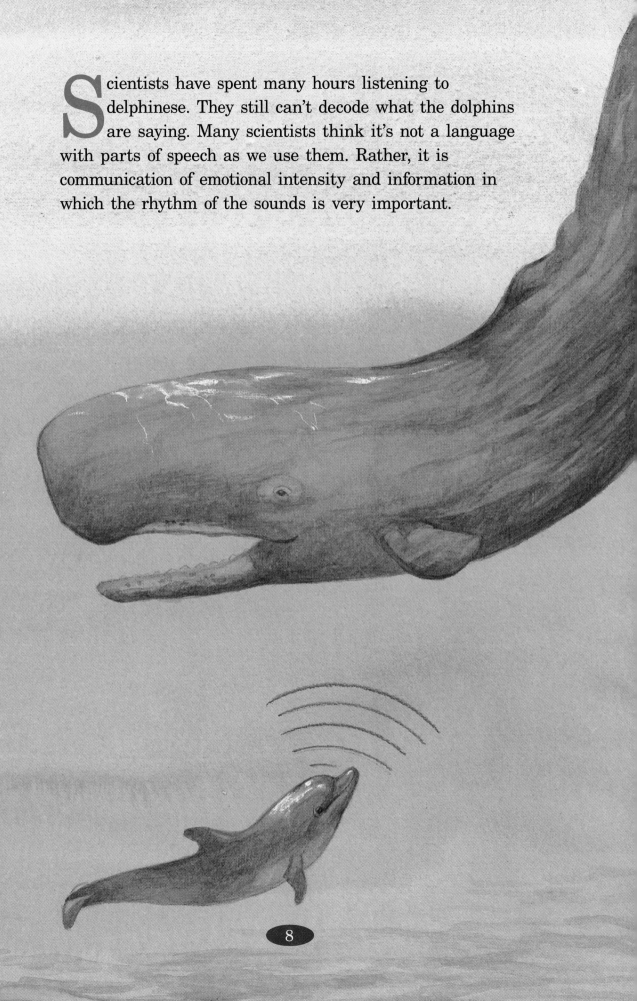

Scientists have spent many hours listening to delphinese. They still can't decode what the dolphins are saying. Many scientists think it's not a language with parts of speech as we use them. Rather, it is communication of emotional intensity and information in which the rhythm of the sounds is very important.

No one knows how dolphins make all of these sounds. Some sounds come from the *blowhole*, an opening on the top of a dolphin's head that it also uses for breathing. Other sounds probably come from their throats. Dolphins have a complex system of air passages throughout their heads. They can even make two sounds at the same time.

One kind of sound has a very special purpose. This is the click. When a group of dolphins takes off on a hunt, they make a series of very fast clicking sounds.

Have they all swallowed clocks like the alligator in Peter Pan? No, they are using dolphin sonar. Dolphins often travel in water that is dark or murky. They can't see where they are going, so they have developed another form of navigation. Instead of using sight, they use sonar.

Sonar is similar to radar. The sound of the click travels through the water. When it hits an object, the sound bounces back to the dolphin like an echo.

Sound travels differently under water. It goes five times faster than it does in the air, and it can also travel for thousands of miles. Dolphins are very sensitive to sound. They have ears, but they receive sound mainly in their foreheads and jaws. When a click bounces back, the dolphin can tell how big and how far away the object is.

A dolphin's sonar is amazingly acute. It can tell whether the object is a rock or a fish. It can even tell if the fish is the tasty kind or not!

Dolphins can make as many as 300 clicks per second. The clicks are high-pitched, much higher then a person can hear. However, you can feel them. If you put your hand in front of a clicking dolphin, you can actually feel the clicks shooting through the water. Swimming next to a dolphin, you might get zapped by a *ping* like a small electric shock. That's the dolphin's sonar checking you out!

The sonar can tell more than just your size and shape. It can see right through your skin and into your body like an x-ray. If a shark is swimming half a mile away, a dolphin's sonar can tell if the shark has a full belly or not. A trained dolphin can even tell the difference in density between metals such as copper and aluminum.

Dolphins have other ways of communicating, too. When they clap their jaws together, it seems to mean that they are angry. Sometimes they send a big bubble through the blowhole. It makes a *gurgle-pop* sound. This seems to be an inquiry, like "What's that?" or "Can I play too?" When a dolphin gets excited, it breathes quickly through its blowhole, producing a *chuff* sound.

Dolphins also use their bodies to communicate. They might shoot up out of the water and come down with a loud smack. This warns other dolphins of danger. When the trainers of a dolphin in captivity see it smack its tail on the water, they knows the dolphin is telling them, "I'm tired of doing that stupid trick!"

Some dolphins have shown that they can learn human words. If a trainer says "tummy," the dolphin will roll over and show its belly. If the trainer says "rock," the dolphin will dive to the bottom of the pool and pick up a rock.

Most trained dolphins read simple hand signals. One hand signal might tell them to do a somersault in the air. Another will ask them to glide across the water on their tails. They can also string together hand signals to do more complex tasks.

One man taught a dolphin to imitate the name he had given her, "Ruby." After a few minutes, the dolphin whistled, "Rooobeee!" with a little bit of a squawk in the middle. The man started jumping up and down. The dolphin repeated "Rooobeee" for a while, then made some other sounds after it. The man imitated the whistles, which sounded like, "Kee-orr-opp."

When the dolphin heard the man say "Kee-orr-opp," he leapt in the air with happiness just as the man had done. The man concluded that the dolphin had just taught him his name in delphinese!

Dolphins are friendly animals. They love to touch each other. They put their flippers across one another's back and rub their beaks together. They swim close beside one another, their bodies brushing together. When dolphins are courting, they bend their bodies into graceful S-shapes to show that they like one another.

There are also many stories of dolphins helping people. They have saved drowning swimmers and guided lost sailors through terrible storms.

Recently dolphins have been used to help people in a new way. In 1971, a disabled boy was brought to some dolphins in a pool. The dolphins were usually rough with visitors, but not with this boy. It seemed that they could tell he was unusual. They swam up to him and stayed very still, then played with him very gently.

Today, many children who have trouble speaking or learning are brought to play with dolphins. After being with the dolphins, some children begin to learn much more quickly. People who have been sick or injured and spend time with dolphins seem to recover more quickly.

No one knows exactly how or why dolphins may help us to learn and heal. We do know that dolphins are wonderful creatures. It makes sense to take care of them just the way they take care of us. But many dolphins are killed every year when they are caught in the nets of commercial fishermen. Others become sick and die from pollution in the marine environment.

If we want to preserve dolphins from these and other dangers, we must be more careful about what we do to their underwater homes. If we do, and if we listen carefully, maybe one day we will learn the meaning of all those squeaks and squawks.

Spotlight Books
Instructional Vocabulary Books
Grade 4

Level 10, Unit 1
Mexican Adventure
City Girl
Trouble at Forest Park
The Pronghorn of the West

Level 10, Unit 2
The Blue Monster
The Grizzly Cub
Sweetbrier Spring Social
Bzzzz-zz! Bees: Friends or Foes?

Level 10, Unit 3
Amanda's Dream
The Angel Food Cake Disaster
Carla's Diary
Fair Play at Fairview

Level 10, Unit 4
Snapdragons
Dolphin Language
Barnabas, The Time Traveler
The Great Eagle "Come-Back"

Level 10, Unit 5
Ballet, Yuck!
A Change of Luck
Blue Teeth
Attack of the Vactors

Level 10, Unit 6
The Lesson
The Case of the Gold Toothpick
Andrew Flies Alone
Sky-High

Spotlight Books
Instructional Vocabulary Books

Macmillan McGraw-Hill

Macmillan/McGraw-Hill
A Division of *The McGraw-Hill Companies*

ISBN 0-02-182215-8 NBZI

99701

9 780021 822157

4, L.10, U.4

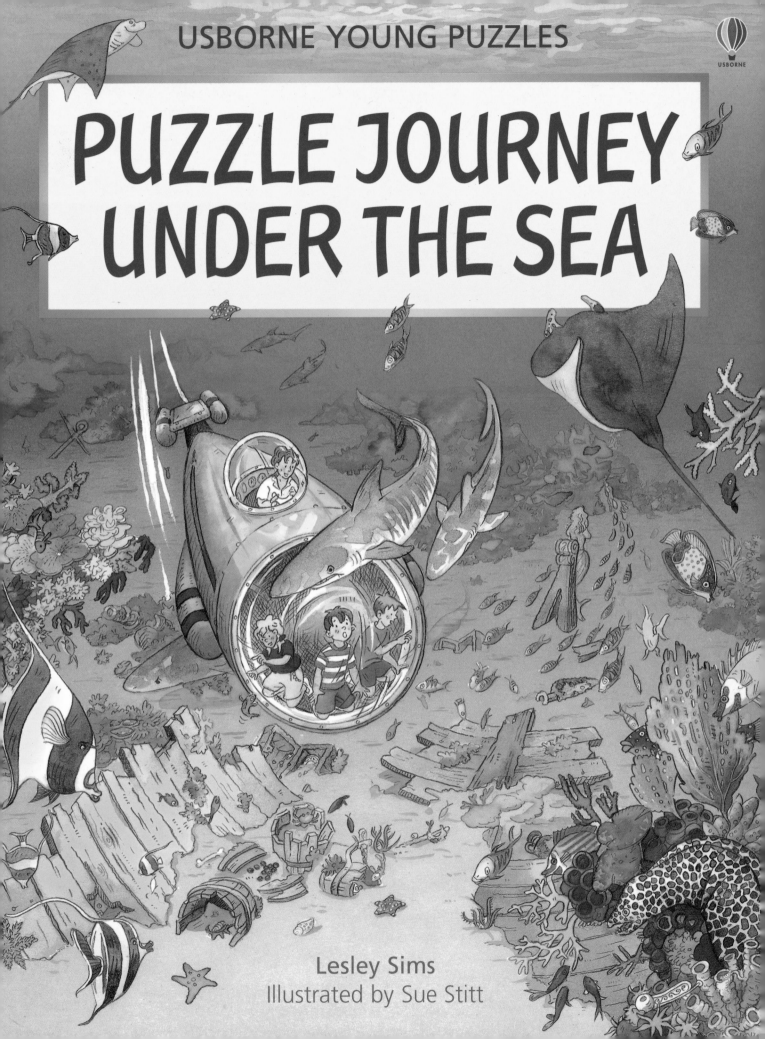

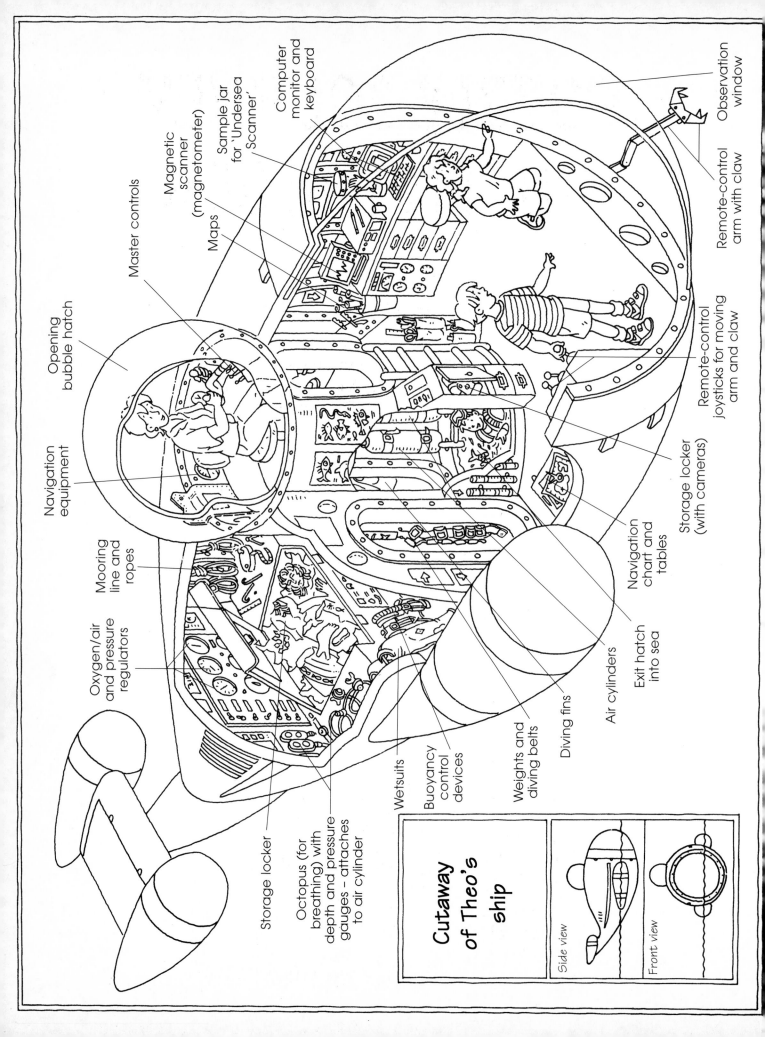

Observation window

Remote-control arm with claw

Computer monitor and keyboard

Sample jar for 'Undersea Scanner'

Magnetic scanner (magnetometer)

Maps

Master controls

Opening bubble hatch

Navigation equipment

Mooring line and ropes

Oxygen/air and pressure regulators

Storage locker

Octopus (for breathing) with depth and pressure gauges – attaches to air cylinder

Wetsuits

Buoyancy control devices

Weights and diving belts

Diving fins

Air cylinders

Exit hatch into sea

Navigation chart and tables

Storage locker (with cameras)

Remote-control joysticks for moving arm and claw

Cutaway of Theo's ship

Side view

Front view